Yarmouth Castle
ISLE OF WIGHT

S E RIGOLD MA, FSA, FRHISTS
formerly Principal Inspector of Ancient Monuments

Part of the coastal defences of Henry VIII, Yarmouth embodied the very latest fashion in military engineering. Completed in 1547, it is square in plan, and washed on two sides by the sea.

During the Civil War the Isle of Wight was strongly royalist and throughout the Commonwealth period Cromwell kept a large garrison here.

When Sir Robert Holmes was appointed Captain of the Island in 1668, the castle was already outmoded and ineffective. He reduced it in size, filled in the moat and built himself a house – now the hotel – on the site.

CONTENTS

Unless otherwise stated illustrations are copyright English Heritage and the photographs were taken by the English Heritage Photographic Section

Visit our website at www.english-heritage.org.uk

Published by English Heritage
1 Waterhouse Square, 138-142 Holborn, London EC1N 2ST
© Crown Copyright 1978
Second edition published by HMSO 1978
First published for English Heritage 1985
Reprinted 1987, 1990, 1992, 1995, 2000, 2003, 2006, 2011
Revised reprint 2012
Printed in England by Pureprint Ltd
06/12 C20, 04815
ISBN 978 1 85074 049 0

DESCRIPTION AND TOUR

Aerial view looking southwest showing Yarmouth Castle at the mouth of the river. It was sited here to protect the vulnerable western part of the island and, with Hurst Castle and Calshot Castle on the mainland, to guard the Solent

Yarmouth Castle is a square with sides of nearly 100ft (30m) and a sharply pointed bastion or flanker at the southeast corner. It differs radically from all the earlier Henry VIII forts, large and small, which have semicircular bastions fronting a higher, central tower.

The north and west walls are washed by the sea; the south and east walls were originally flanked by a moat 30ft (9m) wide, terminated by continuations of the north and west walls, in which there were sluices. The continuation of the west wall, which stands high, can be seen alongside the passenger shelter on the quay.

There was formerly an earthen bulwark of Elizabethan date outside the moat and, more recently, an auxiliary battery on the quay to the west. In the late 17th century the moat was filled in and a house, now the George Hotel, built partly over it. Unfortunately outbuildings of the house still encroach upon the bastion and obscure it. Thus much of the exterior, being closely surrounded by the sea or by private properties, is not accessible, but all can be seen from a distance.

3

Exterior

Bastion

The entrance was originally from the east (see illustration on page 1 and below); the gateway was blocked up when the moat was filled and was unblocked only in the 20th century. It gives on to the garden of the hotel and is not in public use.

Since the late 17th century the entrance has been from the south. Like all Henry VIII's castles, Yarmouth had only one entrance and there was not previously a postern gate in this position. The bastion, which is well seen from the east, over the garden, covered both arms of the moat and thus also covered both the earlier and later entrances. Lateral fire from this position was essential to the defence of the castle and the external masonry of the bastion marries perfectly with that of the curtain wall. It would thus appear to belong to the original build of 1547 and to be the earliest

example of its arrow-head plan in England and one of the earliest in northern Europe.

There were originally no openings in the long sides of the bastion, the one window now visible being of comparatively recent date. The long sides project in short 'ears' and small guns, casemated behind these, provided the lateral fire. The internal construction of the gunports in this position agrees with some, but not all, of the original embrasures elsewhere in the castle. Externally all the embrasures lack the wide splay characteristic of the gunports in the other Henry VIII forts. The lower tiers of guns thus had a limited traverse. There were probably heavier guns on top of the bastion before the domestic roof was put up on it; the embrasures for guns have been expanded to accommodate windows. The original coping of the parapet remains; it is triangular in section, whereas normal Henrician castles have rounded parapets.

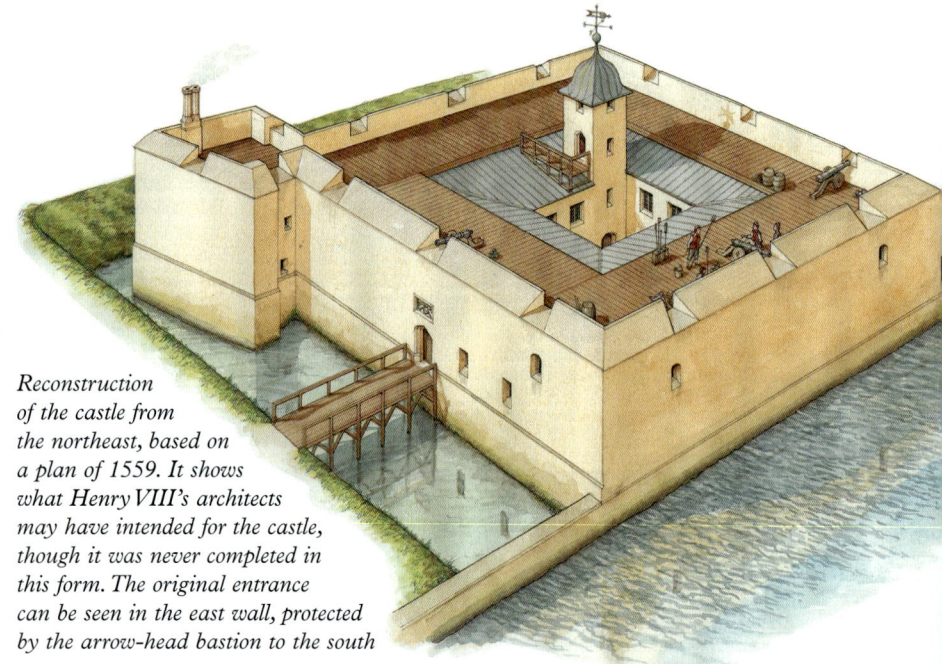

Reconstruction of the castle from the northeast, based on a plan of 1559. It shows what Henry VIII's architects may have intended for the castle, though it was never completed in this form. The original entrance can be seen in the east wall, protected by the arrow-head bastion to the south

Square block

The main armament was always directed towards the sea. Originally the courtyard appears to have been central with a tier of guns set on the upper floor of the surrounding ranges, but from the late 16th century the heaviest guns were mounted on a platform of earth, now occupying the whole northern half of the square. This was originally lower than at present and may not at first have reached the east wall but by the early 17th century had been raised to about its present level, giving an uninterrupted field of fire over the sea, and leaving the curtain walls as blank retaining walls.

The courtyard then occupied the southern half of the square, with a range of buildings along the south wall. These buildings were heightened and enlarged at the end of the 16th century and again in the first half of the 17th.

The unity of the original work is obvious; the same neat ashlar and the same shallow moulded plinth goes right round the castle, though at different levels on the landward and seaward sides.

On the east façade much of the curtain wall survives to the same height as the parapet of the bastion, that is, some 5ft (1.5m) higher than the present parapet of the platform. It presumably continued at this level throughout the east front, but was apparently only four courses higher than the present parapet on the other sides. Most of the additions, above this level belong to the work of *c*1632, characterised by large but less well-fitted ashlar with a peculiar set of masons' marks, the letters E and N and a 'crows-foot' device.

The original entrance gateway on the east side has a four-centred arched head, a broad double chamfer, stopped fairly high, and no visible provision for a drawbridge or portcullis. It is surmounted by the royal arms of Henry VIII, in high stone relief, with a relieving arch above. The crowned shield is surrounded by the

The royal arms of Henry VIII above the original entrance in the east wall of the castle

garter and has the lion and golden dragon for supporters, but there is no other motto or badge. The bold treatment is almost Renaissance in feeling.

Two loops flank the door to the north, principally intended to light a chamber now filled up by the earth of the platform. Their embrasures are roofed internally with flat slabs without smoke vents, and could be used only by bows or hand guns, with very little room for traverse.

On the north side two blocked gunports of the first-floor tier may be seen, one partly masked by a pair of pointed buttresses added in 1609. The buttresses are of good ashlar, with a plain chamfered plinth. The other buttress, on the west side, bears the date and the initial IR for Jacobus Rex (James I); it also covers a blocked gunport of the originally regularly spaced first-floor tier. Nearer the corner is a subsequent patch of repair, dated 1813.

On the west side facing the modern landing stage are two surviving arched gunports of the same tier as the blocked ones, and below them, two small loops like those beside the original entrance. Above the arched gunports can be seen the contrasting masonry of the gable of the long room, added in 1632, with blocked attic windows.

The flanking wall of the moat shows original work below and later courses above, including a characteristic stretch of *c*1632. The same contrast will be noted on

The west wall of the central block, showing two arched gunports and two gun loops beneath them. The walls were raised above the gunports in 1632 to form the gable of the long room

the south side, where the present late 17th-century entrance is reached by a passage. The gateway has a segmental head and low stops, but attempts to blend with the original. The oak doors are modern.

Interior

The breach for the present gate, with a segmental brick head, leads directly into the courtyard through a barrel-vaulted vestibule. This was, in origin, one of the four vaulted compartments made for gunners' lodgings about 1632, carrying the long room above. The arches over the courtyard to the left are of the same date, and this part of the courtyard was formerly covered over and walled off, thus obliging anyone entering to turn right.

Continuing right, with the retaining wall of the platform on the left, visitors should turn into the vestibule of the earlier entrance. Here part of the original brick vault remains, abutted by a 17th- or 18th-century brick vault at a higher level.

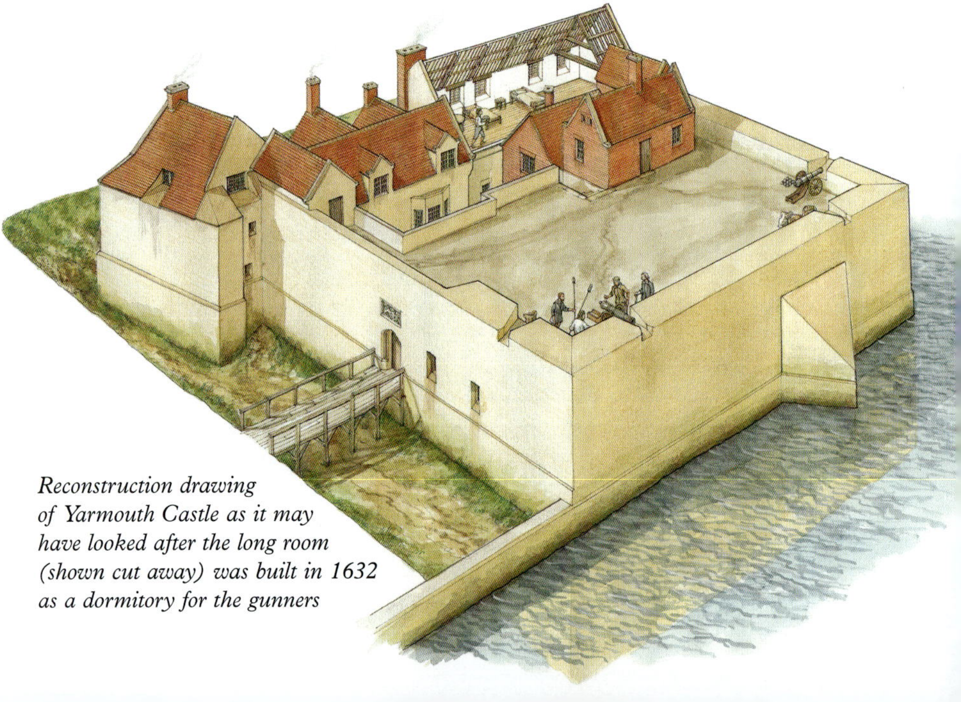

Reconstruction drawing of Yarmouth Castle as it may have looked after the long room (shown cut away) was built in 1632 as a dormitory for the gunners

The master gunner's house and courtyard, seen from the east. The steps on the right lead from the courtyard to the gun platform

Originally the passage seems to have given access to the central courtyard and to a chamber, both now filled with the earth of the platform. The blocking at the end is of neat ashlar, to be associated with the final raising of the platform in 1609, or perhaps a little earlier. Since the latter part of the 16th century, persons entering have had to turn left into the lateral courtyard, keeping the right side against the blank retaining wall.

Returning to the western part of the courtyard, visitors see the master gunner's house on the left. On the right, in the characteristic masonry of *c*1632, is a reinforcement of the retaining wall, perhaps covering a weakness where the central courtyard originally began. At the extreme west end can be seen two square-headed loops and an embrasure, with an arched head, belonging to the main tier, above them. All these openings are mutilated, but the embrasures had brick heads internally, as in the bastion. Those on the right are partly blocked by the platform and its retaining wall. This contains reinforcements and half barrel vaults of 17th-century date, but basically belongs to the same inferior ashlar constructions as the house – that is, when the lateral courtyard was made in the later 16th century.

The narrowness of this end of the courtyard and the rather later blocking of the original entrance passage support the suggestion that the platform originally occupied the northwestern part of the square only. A single barrel vault covers the terminal bay of the courtyard. A small dark cellar, also barrel vaulted, has been fitted into the remaining wall. Perhaps an earlier powder magazine, it was originally also approached through a hatch at high level.

Opposite are the two least altered of the four barrel-vaulted compartments. Both until recently contained circular brick powder magazines, their domes covered with stone flags. These were in existence in 1718 and are part of Holmes' improvements, or perhaps a little later.

The western magazine, being very ruinous, was removed to show the state of the compartment before its insertion. Entrance is through the original iron-reinforced door of the pair of magazines, and a wooden doorcase in a brick surround, connecting the pair, leads to the now gutted end compartment. Both compartments had a door, a window and a fireplace on each floor, the fireplace set obliquely, in the 17th-century fashion. There are remains of plaster of the same date, on the much patched walls.

A deep brick locker has been made in the blocked gunport of the main tier on the first floor. Below ground was a small square cellar. The upper doors are now fitted with iron grills.

On the other side of the entrance vestibule, formerly the third compartment of lodgings, is the fourth compartment, altered in the 19th century and united with the house. The communicating doors have now been blocked and removal of later work shows a pair of corner fireplaces, a door and window on the upper floor and a segmental barrel vault as in the others. The altered ground-floor door is set askew. There is an original loop on this floor, with

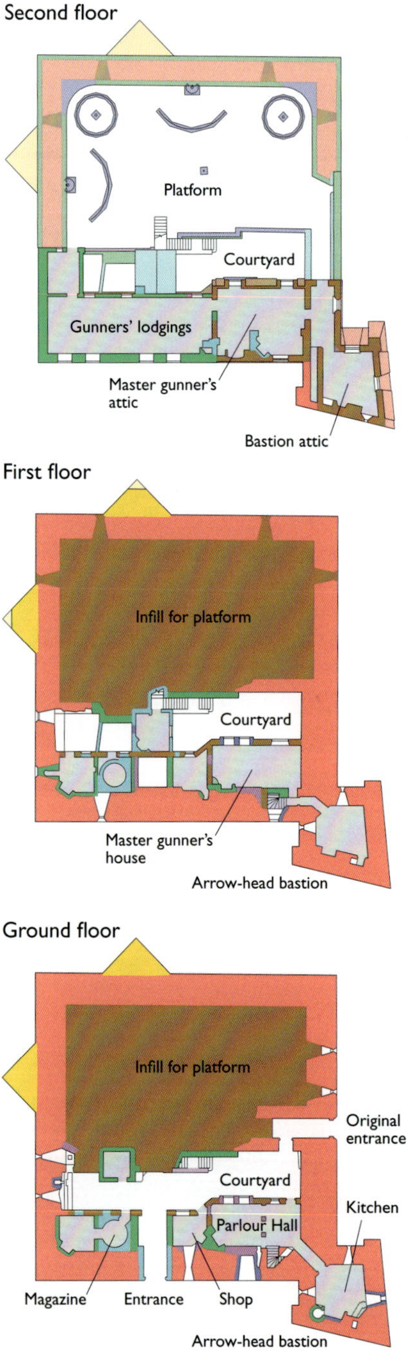

Second floor

Platform

Courtyard

Gunners' lodgings

Master gunner's
attic

Bastion attic

First floor

Infill for platform

Courtyard

Master gunner's
house

Arrow-head bastion

Ground floor

Infill for platform

Original
entrance

Courtyard

Kitchen

Parlour Hall

Magazine   Entrance   Shop

Arrow-head bastion

a relatively wide and deep outer splay and
internal covering of stone slabs, as in
smaller loops beside the original entrance.
A similar embrasure, very mutilated, can
be traced to the east of this, in the house.

Master gunner's house

This was originally of two storeys; the
better finished top storey was added at the
end of the 16th century, or possibly as
late as 1609. The bastion, however, may
have received its top storey and span roof
in the first building. It is a good example
of an Elizabethan house plan, of medieval
derivation: the door led into a truncated
hall, communicating with a kitchen and
service wing, which was formed in the
bastion, and a large and well-lighted
parlour on the side away from the door.
This three-fold division was repeated on
the upper floor.

The screen wall between the hall and
parlour existed in the 18th century, but its
position is now shown by two stone piers.
The house retained its original bay
windows in the parlour and chamber above
until the present plain flush windows were
inserted in the early 19th century.

The roof line of the former lean-to porch
can be seen. The door has a four-centred
head, its chamfer stopped low. The hall
window beside it has its original mullion.
The staircase rises from the hall in the
thickness of the wall, a normal position in
the 17th century, but perhaps replacing an
earlier wooden stair. In the much repaired
south wall, formerly breached by an early

Floor plans of Yarmouth Castle

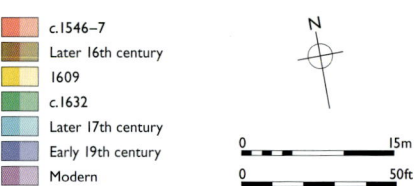

▧	c.1546–7
▧	Later 16th century
▧	1609
▧	c.1632
▧	Later 17th century
▧	Early 19th century
▧	Modern

N

0   15m
0   50ft

The master gunner's kitchen on the ground floor of the bastion. It was recorded in 1623 as 'the captaines kuchin, covered with straw, verie daungerous by reason of sparks of ffyre that fly from the ordenance'

19th-century doorway, are traces of an original loop and the restored parlour fireplace has a wooden lintel.

In the kitchen, approached by the original passage, vaulted in brick like the gun embrasures and leading to a square-headed stone door, are the two small gunports that covered the moat from the bastion. One is blocked, but the brick heads, finished in ashlar and provided with smoke vents, are well preserved. A late window has been forced in the side wall to improving lighting. Beside the kitchen fireplace, with its massive wooden lintel, is a brick baker's oven. In the corner is a drain or garderobe pit, grooved for a penstock, and belonging to the original construction, though useful as a domestic drain for the kitchen.

The staircase leads to the chambers over the hall, made into one. There is little to note here except a 17th-century fireplace with a plain chamfer, and beams with ovolo, or quarter-round, mouldings and bar stops, no doubt added with the floor above, but of different pattern from the beams in the chamber on this floor in the bastion. These have remarkable leaf-shaped stops, found also on the trusses of the attic above.

This chamber, approached from the stair-head by a four-centred arch, leading into a bent brick-vaulted passage, is the finest in the house. Besides another pair of gun embrasures, like those below, it has a good four-centred arched fireplace with high stops and brick relieving arch, and a small brick-vaulted garderobe chamber or privy in the corner, with a square-headed door.

There were formerly two staircases to the uppermost floor, but this can now be approached only from the platform. Entering from the vestibule at the east end of the platform, with a two-light 16th-century window, visitors pass through a doorway, altered from a very short oblique passage, into the attic of the bastion. The windows are remade, but a small, blocked stone window in the gable perhaps served a screened-off garderobe. The fireplace has a plain, wooden lintel.

The roof with scalloped principal rafters and leaf stops is markedly superior to that in the attic over the hall and parlour, approached from the same vestibule. This has a series of dormer windows and a 17th-century fireplace shows the position of a former brick partition. Beside the plain fireplace in the farther room is a locker. The roof is a rough but massive construction with plain collar beams. The attic leads directly into the long room.

Long room

This dates from *c*1632, and follows closely on the building of the four barrel vaults on which it stands. The end gable of the adjoining attic can be traced, embedded in the larger gable of the long room. Adjoining this are the remains of the various flues from the rooms below. The lower course of the long room is composed of the original ashlar of the curtain wall. Above this is

miscellaneous work of *c*1632. The typical external ashlar is backed by irregular stone and brick, but the north wall is of neat brickwork and comparatively thin.

The windows are renewed and later accretions have been removed, leaving a plain but light room, now used for exhibition purposes. In the floor are two glazed covers. One shows the deep embrasure of a main tier gunport, faced with ashlar; the covering vault, long ago removed, was probably of brick. The other shows a rough and mutilated medieval carving of an archbishop with a cross staff, reused in the barrel vault below. It was probably a corbel and ultimately derives from a monastic building.

The massive roof with tie beams and collar is original. There was once a loft carried on the ties and lighted by the small windows, now blocked, in the north gable. A second vestibule, showing well the contrast between the thin brickwork and the massive ashlar of *c*1632, leads back to the platform at the west end.

The parlour on the ground floor of the master gunner's house, dressed as it may have looked in the first half of the 17th century

Two small two-roomed lodgings were constructed to replace those put out of action by the formation of the present entrance and magazines. One was carried on arches over the courtyard and one room of it survives as the custodian's office. The blocked communicating door to the other room remains. The floor was below the platform level. The other apartment, now quite demolished, stood beside the steps on top of the platform.

Platform

This was constructed between 1559-65, to carry all the heavier armament of the castle. The parapet, now covered by a turf capping, dates from one of the 17th-century alterations – probably that of 1632, when the already blocked original gunports were largely masked by a new facing both within and without.

The rounded internal angles were formed in 1813, when the date-marked repair was made to the outer face. The iron rails, on which the gun carriages were traversed, correspond with the rounded angles and seem to belong to the same scheme, though the last fitting-out with fresh guns was as late as 1855.

Before 1813 there were more, but less manoeuvrable guns, and the coping of the parapet sloped down to the vertical face. But the level and the general appearance of the platform has been unaltered since the early 17th century, except that it was formerly paved all over. The slight mutilations of the inner parapet face were caused by the latest gun mountings.

The wide view shows that it was a most advantageous position. In detail, its function evolved slowly, as the range and mobility of artillery improved. Originally a tier of seven or eight guns in arched embrasures offered point-blank fire at short range, as on a battleship. The making and raising of the platform allowed for eight guns with uninterrupted fire. Finally this was achieved by four guns with a longer and wider range.

Gun platform from the northwest, showing one of the buttresses of 1609 in the foreground

HISTORY

In 1538 King Henry VIII, troubled by a *rapprochement* between his potential enemies, the Holy Roman Emperor and the King of France, ordered a series of castles and blockhouses, fitted for artillery, to be built at vulnerable points along the east and south coasts of England. These included Calshot and Hurst Castles, on spits off the mainland shore of the Solent, and two 'Cow Towers,' flanking the Medina (whence the name Cowes). There was as yet no fort at Yarmouth, but an earlier round tower had been built by Sir James Worsley at Sharpnode Point, more than 1 mile (1.6km) to the west. This and 'Carey's Sconce,' that later supplemented it, were replaced by forts in Victorian days.

By 1543 the castles were nearing completion, but the original threat had now passed and Henry renewed his alliance with the Emperor. This brought a fresh war with France. On the whole the English fared the better and captured Boulogne. But in 1545, while the King was actually at Portsmouth, the French sailed into the Solent, keeping out of reach of coastal and naval guns, and then landed simultaneously at three points on the southwest shore of the Isle of Wight, including Sandown, where an additional castle had just been begun. The local militia, under the Captain of the Island, Richard Worsley, son of Sir James, rose to the occasion, drove the invaders back to the ships and killed one of their

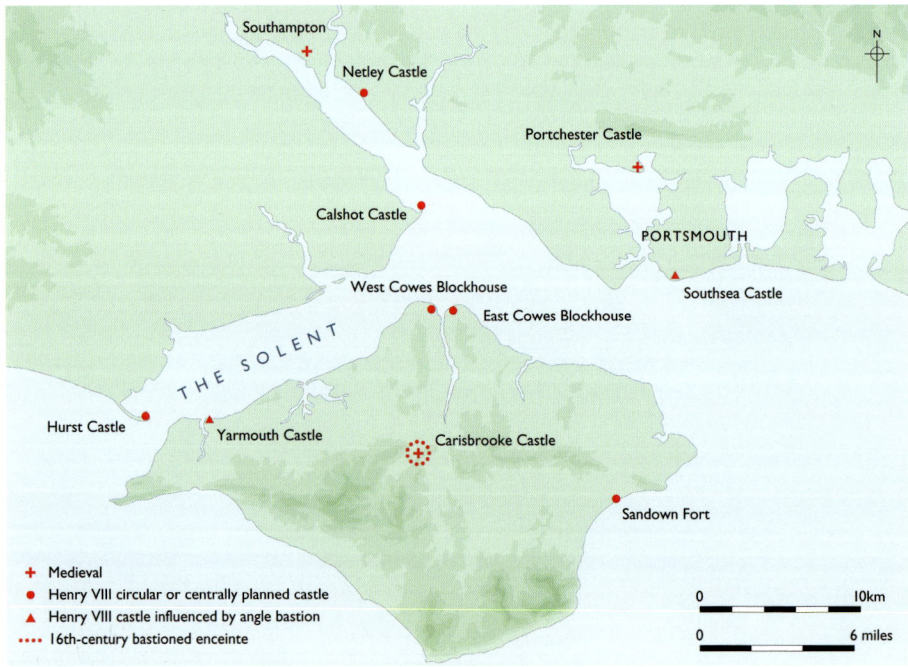

Map showing the key strongholds around the Solent in the 16th century. This area was a focus for Henry VIII's defence-building programme, to protect the naval anchorage at Portsmouth

commanders. The French had harried far into the island, but did not reach Yarmouth. The tradition that the castle occupies the site of a church destroyed on that occasion would seem properly to refer to an earlier raid, in which Yarmouth was burnt, in the time of Richard II.

The original system of castles having thus proved inadequate, Sandown was forthwith finished and armed, and a new fort undertaken at Yarmouth, a vulnerable position and the main point of communication between the western part of the Island and the mainland. The castle was built on the 'King's land,' outside the jurisdiction of the borough.

Yarmouth Castle was considered serviceable by September 1547, when £1000 was paid to George Mills for building works and for the discharge of the soldiers guarding operations. It then contained three cannon and culverins (see the glossary) and twelve smaller guns. At the same time every parish on the island was required to possess a gun and a team to man it. Some of these guns still survive. The guiding spirit of these defences was Richard Worsley, the Captain, who 'put the people in warlike array for the increase of haquebusry' (musketry) and was clearly an able and strenuous 'territorial' soldier.

This was a period of rapid progress in military engineering. The castles conceived in 1538 all had low round bastions to carry the guns. By 1545 these were being superseded, not only in Italy, but as near as Antwerp, by pointed or 'arrow-head' bastions, which allowed complete coverage of the walls by lateral fire with minimum exposure. At first something of a secret, the system became generally known after P Cattaneo published a book on it in 1554.

Yarmouth Castle has one arrow-head bastion, as had the original Sandown. This bastion was in existence in 1559 and is shown on a survey plan of that date, made under Worsley's supervision, and now belonging to the Earl of Dartmouth. The plan was discovered by Mr J D Jones, Curator of Carisbrooke Castle Museum. A bastion in this position was required from the beginning and the general plan of Yarmouth Castle is radically different from that of the castles of 1538. It can be confidently inferred that the bastion dates from the original construction of 1546–47, and is thus the earliest of its kind in England by a dozen years.

Extensive fortifications of this pattern were begun at Berwick-upon-Tweed in 1558 under professional engineers, Sir Richard Lee and Richard Popinjay, who had previously served at Portsmouth, but Worsley himself had mastered the newest principles of gunnery and fortification sufficiently to be consulted on the defences of Portsmouth in 1558 and, later, on those of the Channel Islands. It is impossible to ascribe the design of Yarmouth to any of these engineers in particular. Nevertheless, it can legitimately be regarded as a forerunner of Berwick.

Worsley was dismissed by Queen Mary I in 1553, in favour of a man of little competence and a Roman Catholic, one Girling, later arrested for robbing the Treasury. Worsley was recalled in 1558 by Queen Elizabeth I, and subsequently restored to the Captaincy. Immediately all the castles in the island were survey-ed, repaired and improved. When Worsley died in 1565, having never even received the knighthood that his office usually carried and his services certainly deserved, a large sum was owing to him by the Crown for works at Carisbrooke and Yarmouth, for the 'placing of the Ordnance,' at his own expenses – a typical example of Queen Elizabeth's 'economy.' This must refer to the creation of the platform on the seaward side of Yarmouth and the abandonment of the central courtyard, which is shown on

Detail of a map of the northeast coast of the Isle of Wight in 1718 by Clement Lempriere, showing Yarmouth Castle. The town of Yarmouth was at one time surrounded by sea and the causeway built to link it to the land to the south (top) can be seen on this map

the plan of 1559, in favour of a lateral one, as Worsley recommended in his survey. The existing house was begun about this date. Worsley left two young sons, who, by the irony of fate, were killed in an accident with gunpowder.

Under Richard Udall, the first captain of the castle (not to be confused with the Captain, that is, the Governor of the Island) the garrison comprised a master gunner, a porter and seventeen soldiers. Later, except during the Commonwealth period, the number of ordinary gunners never exceeded four or five. The stone house, of indifferent ashlar, flanking the courtyard and probably built before 1565, was possibly intended for the captain but later used by the master gunner. There were further chambers in the same range, not necessarily for the garrison, which at first was probably billeted outside.

In the later Elizabethan and Jacobean periods, the castle underwent frequent modifications. In 1587, when the Spanish Armada was imminent, some £50 worth of repairs was done, and in 1597–98, when Spain had lost much of the initiative in the war, a more elaborate addition was made. Besides further repairs and a new building on the platform, which, hitherto at least, was lower than at present, an earthen bulwark, with bastions and revelins for further guns, was constructed outside the moat. All these ramparts have now disappeared, but they were typical of the artillery fortifications of the period, frequently added to earlier curtain walls, and well seen, for instance, at Carisbrooke.

In 1599 Sir Edward Uvedale stressed the strategic importance of the castle and pressed for further and costly repairs, which were reported almost complete in

1603. Finally in 1609, the year of the last charter to the borough, there were further repairs, which, with work at Sandown, cost £300. These included a length of new seawall to protect the moat and the two corner buttresses of neat ashlar, one of which bears the date and the cipher of King James I. These buttresses partly mask the old gunports of the platform, which was therefore raised to its present height, either then or in one of the preceding campaigns of repair. A top storey, also of fine stone-work, was added to the house about the same time.

Three separate operations in twelve years ought to have secured the castle for a long period. Nevertheless in 1623 a further survey revealed bad conditions: the parapet in the Middle Tower (the stone castle rather than the outer earthworks) was decayed; the sluice to the moat, as usual, was out of order; and lodging was wanted for four gunners, indicating that it was now desired to house them inside.

The author of this report, John Burley, was captain of the castle, and two others of his name succeeded him in office. They were staunch Royalists and the Captain Burley, who made an attempt to rescue Charles I from Carisbrooke, was probably of the same family.

No immediate action was taken on the report, nor on further suggestions in 1625 and 1629, when the proposals included a half-moon battery. But the military value of the castle was well appreciated at this time, when there was war, first with Spain and subsequently with the French king, on behalf of the Huguenots.

Yarmouth was frequently mentioned in official reports as a seat of communication, a depot for stores and, once, for the transit of troops – a Scots regiment, some of whom were stationed there and made themselves very unpopular. Finally, in 1632, a considerable sum of money was allocated.

After Sandown, which had been ruined by the sea, had been rebuilt as a perfect example of a square fort with four arrow-head bastions, work was begun at Yarmouth in accordance with the recommendations of 1623. Partition walls carrying barrel vaults, in the range to the west of the house, provided four cramped little lodgings with fireplaces on both storeys. More rooms were carried on arches over the courtyard. The revetment of the platform was reinforced, the parapet raised, and finally, perhaps after a short interval, a long room was created over the barrel vaults, originally a store for provisions and tackle, serving the platform, rather than a barrackroom. The work of this period is recognisable by massive and often weathered masonry bearing a peculiar set of masons' marks. Coupled with the ecclesiastical carving in the barrel vaults, this suggests secondary re-use and the stone may derive from the destroyed Sandown.

The Civil War in 1642 found the local gentry and all the castle commanders Royalist. Captain Barnaby Burley was prepared to hold Yarmouth for the King, even with his minute garrison. Then, with more discretion, he surrendered on condition that he continued in command and had sufficient guard. In due course he was replaced and the island remained securely in Parliamentarian hands.

By 1650 the garrison had grown to thirty men and it was proposed to add thirty more and a lieutenant. In the same year all the castles in the island were overhauled, Parliament being still unsure of victory, as Prince Charles was threatening them from Jersey. In 1654 there were seventy men, most of them necessarily billeted outside, but all perhaps needed to man the guns fully, which in the time of the Dutch Wars still included a battery on the outer bulwarks to the east.

Drawing of Yarmouth Castle by Charles Tomkins, 1794. A soldier patrols on the castle gun platform and on the right can be seen one of the guns of the battery on the quay (now gone), built by Robert Holmes or his heir in the late 17th century

With the Restoration of 1660 came a swift disbanding of the swollen army. In 1661 the garrison of Yarmouth, still probably seventy, was dismissed at four days' notice and the guns were ordered to be removed unless the townsmen would man them themselves. This they declined to do, but it was evidently intended to revert to the arrangement prevailing before 1642, with a small garrison and the duty of handling the numerous guns must have rested with the local militia.

After some years of uncertainty, Sir Robert Holmes, an English naval veteran born in Ireland and appointed Captain of the Island in 1668, undertook to reorganise defence on his own initiative. By then the garrison of four gunners had returned, probably because they were claiming the living as a perquisite they or their fathers had enjoyed before the war, but they had no officer. Holmes recovered what guns he could store at Cowes and reduced the castle to manageable size by demolishing the earthworks and filling in the moat.

When the ground had settled Holmes, or perhaps his heir, built a house (rebuilt in the early 18th century and now the George Hotel) on the edge of the moat. The old entrance was blocked, a new entrance made on the south side, and all the guns concentrated on the seaward side, supplemented by a new battery, now quite obliterated, on the quay. Sir Robert was anxious to hold the castle for King James II, but both garrison and populace prevented him by declaring for William of Orange. Holmes died in 1692 and has a fine monument in St James's Church, Yarmouth.

Monument in St James's Church, Yarmouth, to Sir Robert Holmes (c1622–1692). Holmes was appointed Captain of the Isle of Wight in December 1668

Yarmouth in 1838, showing boats at high tide sailing near the castle walls

A boat being pulled up the beach out of a rough sea at Yarmouth in about 1830. Three chimneys of what is now the George Hotel, can be seen behind the castle

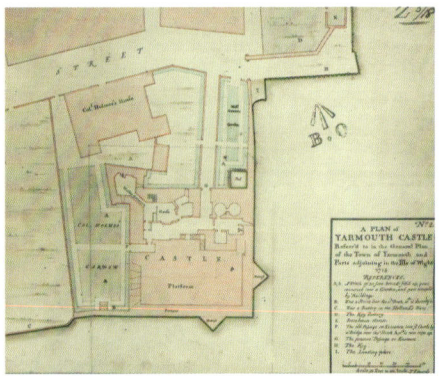

Above, the 1718 survey of the castle, and below, the survey of about 1760. Gardens and Sir Robert Holmes's house have replaced the moat which surrounded the castle in the previous century

Thus reinstated, the castle remained as a quite little establishment throughout the 18th century. Surveys of 1718 and about 1760 show no change (see left and below); there were eight 6-pounder guns on the platform and five 9-pounders on the quay battery. The garrison in 1781, and doubtless throughout the period, comprised a captain, a master gunner and five gunners – not nearly enough to man the ordnance without the local militia. Even in 1795, when the great Revolutionary Wars had begun, they were still no more. In fact the castle was regarded as ineffective and to this it owes its preservation.

There were repairs in 1813, towards the end of the Napoleonic Wars, and the parapet, which had previously had a more sloping profile, reached its present form. At the same time the present rails, or

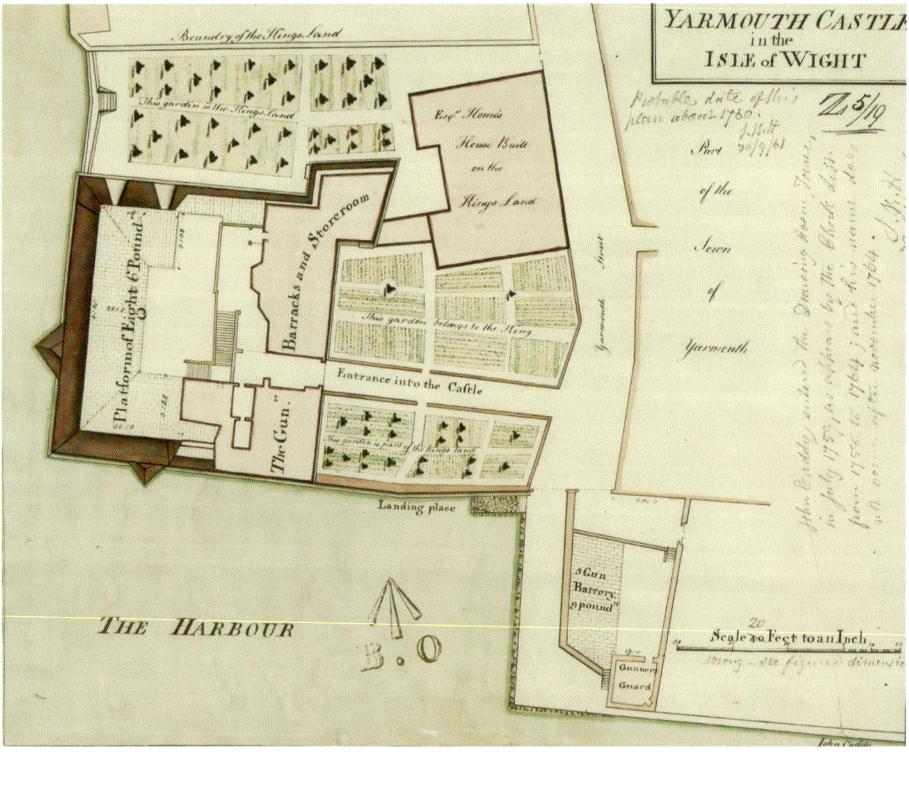

YARMOUTH CASTLE in the ISLE of WIGHT

THE HARBOUR

'racers,' were laid down to take the traversing platforms of four guns of naval type, the only remaining armament. The same small establishment continued into the 19th century until in 1881 the authorities considered a plan for thorough modernisation, which fortunately for archaeology, they dropped, and in 1885 they decided to withdraw the garrison and dismantle the guns which had been renewed thirty years before.

The castle remained in the hands of the War Department, though only used by the coastguard for signalling, until 1901, when it was transferred to the Commissioners of Woods and Forests. These transferred it to what is now the Department of the Environment in 1913, when some repairs were undertaken. It was partially commandeered for service

Yarmouth harbour in about 1900, when the castle was still in the hands of the War Department and used for signalling by the coastguard

use in both World Wars and occupation of some of the rooms by ex-service and other organisations delayed complete rehabilitation until the 1950s. Since 1984 Yarmouth Castle has been in the care of English Heritage.

View of the harbour and castle in 1938. The breakwater, which narrowed the entrance to the harbour, was built in 1847

GLOSSARY

Ashlar Squared blocks of stone; dressed masonry of large blocks laid in regular courses with fine joints

Barrel vault Vault with a semicylindrical vault; tunnel vault

Bastion Projection from the outer walls of a castle or fortification from which the garrison can see, and defend by flanking fire, the ground before the ramparts

Bulwark Bastion or (in first half of 16th century) a blockhouse; rampart; defensive wall

Buttress Masonry projection from a wall or the corner of a building to give additional strength or to resist the lateral thrust of an arch or roof

Casemate Vaulted room with embrasures, built into the thickness of the ramparts or other fortifications and used as a barracks or battery or both; vaulted chamber in the thickness of a wall; well-protected vault under a rampart, normally used as a gun emplacement and/or for accommodation for the garrison; vaulted chamber in the thickness of an outer wall with embrasures for shooting through

Chamfer Bevelled or mitred edge, formed by cutting off the arris usually at 45 degrees

Corbel Stone or wooden projection from a wall to support a beam, etc

Culverin Large cannon, very long in proportion to its bore

Curtain wall Defensive enclosure wall often connecting one tower with another

Embrasure Opening in a wall, usually splayed internally, for admitting light or shooting through; also used as the equivalent of crenellation (opening in the upper part of a parapet; battlement)

Garderobe Latrine usually flushed by a channel of water or by discharging into a cesspit or through an outer wall

Loop, loophole Narrow vertical slit in a wall, deeply splayed within to increase the angle of vision and/or the amount of light admitted, through which defenders shot with bows or guns (hence *arrow loop, gun loop*)

Mullion Length of stone, wood or metal dividing a window or other opening vertically into two or more lights. *Transom* is the horizontal member

Ovolo Convex moulding of quarter-circle or quarter-ellipse section, receding downwards

Penstock Sluice or floodgate

Plinth Projecting masonry at the base of a wall or column, often chamfered (q.v.) or with decorative mouldings

Rampart Bank of earth or rock usually derived from the excavation of an outer ditch surrounding a fortified enclosure

Ravelin Fortified island in the moat in front of a curtain wall

Revetment Retaining wall built to support or hold back a mass of earth or water

Scalloped Shaped in a series of curves or scallops